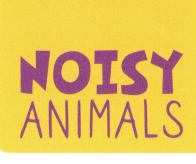

Say "Hello!" in the Jungle

By Madeline Tyler

www.littlebluehousebooks.com

Copyright © 2025 by Little Blue House, Mendota Heights, MN 55120. All rights reserved. No part of this book may be reproduced or utilized in any form or by any means without written permission from the publisher.

Little Blue House is distributed by North Star Editions:
sales@northstareditions.com | 888-417-0195

Library of Congress Control Number: 2024936703

ISBN
979-8-89359-007-4 (hardcover)
979-8-89359-017-3 (paperback)
979-8-89359-037-1 (ebook pdf)
979-8-89359-027-2 (hosted ebook)

Printed in the United States of America
Mankato, MN
082024

Written by: Madeline Tyler

Edited by: Robin Twiddy

Designed by: Jasmine Pointer

QR by: Kelby Twyman

All facts, statistics, web addresses and URLs in this book were verified as valid and accurate at time of writing. No responsibility for any changes to external websites or references can be accepted by either the author or publisher.

To use the QR codes in this book, a grown-up will need to set one of these apps as the default browser on the device you are using:

. Chrome
. Safari
. Firefox
. Ecosia

Image & Sound Credits
All images courtesy of Shutterstock.com. With thanks to Getting Images, Thinkstock Photo, and iStockphoto.

All sounds (s) by http://soundbible.com. Character – Lorelyn Medina . Front Cover - romawka, Studio_G, Gaidamashchuk, VectorShow. 3 – Quick Shot. 4 – 5 – Vidoslava. 6 – Pumidol, Daniel Simon (s). 7 – Maquiladora. 8 – Oriol Querol, Mike Koenig (s). 9 – Maquiladora. 10 – Grigorii Pisotsckii. 11 – Spreadthesign. 12 – marktucan, Mike Koenig (s). 13 – Gaidamashchuk, GraphicsRF. 14 – Karel Bartik. 15 – Maquiladora. 16 – Tanguy de Saint-Cyr, Caroline Ford (s). 17 – Maquiladora, Pretty Vectors. 18 – Ondrej Prosicky. 19 – Maquiladora. 20 – GUDKOV ANDREY. 21 – MarySan. 22 – Vaclav Sebek, Lisa Redfern (s). 23 – Maquiladora.

Your QR app might open the links in this book right away. If it doesn't, tap the button that says "open," "continue," "browse," or something similar.

Lots of animals live in the jungle. It can get very noisy!

Scan the QR code to hear the noises of the jungle.

Gibbons use their long arms to swing from branch to branch.

Scan the QR code to hear the gibbons say "hello."

This elephant has a long trunk that it uses to breathe.

Scan the QR code to hear the elephant say "hello."

8

Piranhas live in some rivers in South America. They have very sharp teeth.

Can you say "hello" like a piranha?

10

Snap, snap, snap!

Jaguars can swim in rivers and climb tall trees.

Scan the QR code to hear the jaguar say "hello."

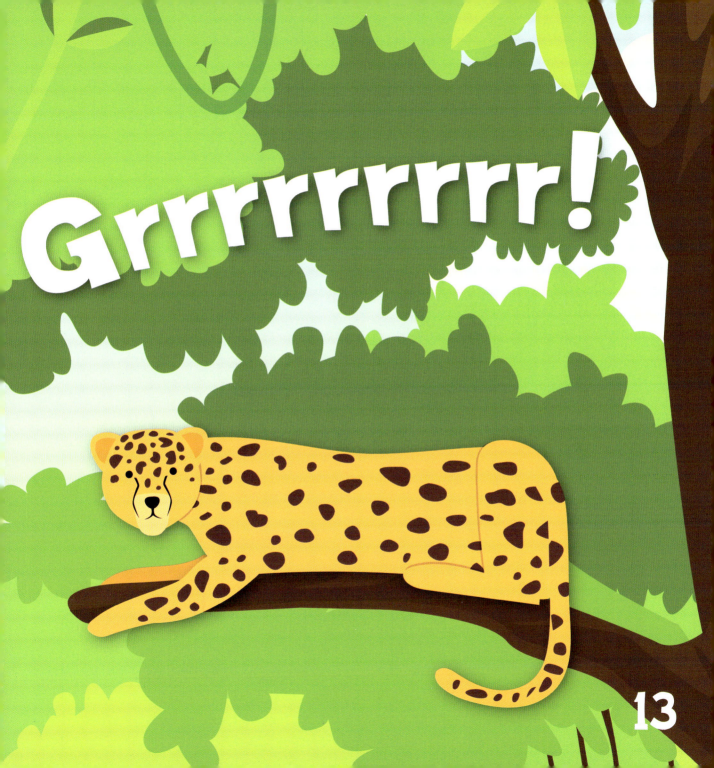

A group of hippos is called a school.

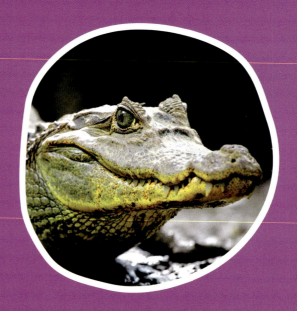

Caimans have hard, strong scales all over their bodies that protect them from harm.

Scan the QR code to hear the caiman say "hello."

16

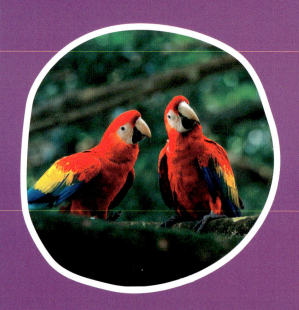

Macaws are very chatty. Their squawks and screams can be heard throughout the jungle!

Scan the QR code to hear the macaw say "hello."

In the wild, ring-tailed lemurs are only found on an island called Madagascar.

There are lots of different types of frogs. Some are spotty, and some are stripy. Nearly all of them are bright and colorful.

Scan the QR code to hear the frogs say "hello."